D1320518

Amazing Adventures

Written by Simon Adams
Reading consultants: Christopher Collier and Alan Howe,
Bath Spa University, UK

This edition published by Parragon in 2013

Parragon
Chartist House,
15-17 Trim Street
Bath, BA1 1HA, UK
www.parragon.com

Copyright © Parragon Books Ltd 2012
Please retain this information for future reference.

©2012 Discovery Communications, LLC. Discovery Kids,
DiscoveryFacts, and related logos and indicia are trademarks
of Discovery Communications, LLC, used under license.
All rights reserved. *discoverykids.com*

All rights reserved. No part of this publication may be reproduced,
stored in a retrieval system, or transmitted, in any form or by any means,
electronic, mechanical, photocopying, recording, or otherwise, without
the prior permission of the copyright holder.

ISBN 978-1-4723-1770-4

Printed in China

Discovery KIDS™

Amazing Adventures

PaRRagon

Bath • New York • Singapore • Hong Kong • Cologne • Delhi
Melbourne • Amsterdam • Johannesburg • Shenzhen

Put on your 3D glasses and prepare for a close encounter. The adventures look so real, you will want to reach out and touch them!

Parents' Notes

This book is part of a series of nonfiction books designed to appeal to children learning to read.

Each book has been developed with the help of educational experts.

At the end of the book is a quiz to help your child remember the information and the meanings of some of the words and sentences. Difficult words, which appear in bold in the book, can be found in the glossary at the back. There is also an index.

Contents

The Vikings

The Vikings, or Norsemen, were early explorers. They came from Denmark, Norway, and Sweden. Between the years 800 and 1400, they set sail in search of new lands to live in.

Crossing the oceans in a Viking boat was very dangerous. The Vikings found their way across the oceans using only the sun and stars to navigate.

Viking boat

The Vikings made new homes in Ireland, Scotland, the Faroe Islands, Iceland, Greenland, and Canada. They built villages like the ones they had come from.

Viking village

DISCOVERY FACT™

The Vikings were the first **Europeans** to visit North America. Leif Eriksson visited in about the year 1000.

A replica of a Viking boat

Gobi Desert

DISCOVERY FACT™

Marco Polo was Niccolo's son. He was just 17 years old when he left Italy.

The Polos

In the 1200s, Niccolo, Maffeo, and Marco Polo traveled from Venice, in Italy, to China. At that time, travel to other lands was difficult and often dangerous.

On their way to China, the Polos had to cross the Gobi Desert. It was very dangerous.

Kublai Khan

The Polos visited Kublai Khan. He was an emperor in China. They wanted to trade with his wealthy **empire**.

Marco Polo lived in China for 20 years. He worked for Kublai Khan and traveled in China and Asia. Eventually, he returned to Italy.

9

Portuguese Explorers

Between 1400 and 1500, Portuguese explorers sailed from Europe to India and China. They sailed around Africa and across the Indian Ocean.

DISCOVERY FACT™

The Portuguese invented a new kind of ship called a caravel. It was good at surviving storms.

In 1488, Bartolomeu Dias and his crew were the first men to sail around the southern tip of Africa, the Cape of Good Hope.

In 1497–99, Vasco da Gama and his crew were the first men to sail from Europe to India and back again.

Bartolomeu Dias

Vasco da Gama

Cape of Good Hope

A replica of the
Santa Maria

Discovering the Americas

In 1492, Christopher Columbus discovered the Americas by accident. He was actually trying to sail to Asia!

Columbus

Columbus set sail from Palos, Spain, with three ships: the Niña, the Santa Maria, and the Pinta.

Columbus discovered Cuba and Haiti. But he believed he had landed in India!

New fruit and vegetables were discovered in the Americas, such as pineapples, potatoes, and corn.

Pineapple

DISCOVERY FACT™

There were already people living in the Americas when Columbus landed. He met a tribe called the Arawaks.

Sailing Around the World

In 1522, Ferdinand Magellan's crew were the first people to sail around the world.

While on his voyage, Magellan was the first European to see a species of penguin on the coast of South America. They were named Magellan penguins after the explorer.

Magellan

Magellan died on the voyage in a battle in the Philippines. Magellan's crew went on without him. The voyage took them three years. Only 17 out of 250 men survived. Magellan set off with five Spanish ships, but only one ship, the Victoria, made it home.

The Victoria

DISCOVERY FACT™

Magellan did not mean to sail around the world. He was trying to sail to Asia to buy spices, such as the ones in this picture.

Magellan penguins

Discovering Australia and New Zealand

Europeans discovered Australia and New Zealand in the 1600s and 1700s. However, other explorers had discovered these lands long before.

Aboriginal boy

Polynesian boat

About 40,000 years ago, the **Aborigines** walked from Asia to Australia across land that today is underneath the sea.

In about the year 1000, **Polynesian** explorers discovered New Zealand.

Between 1642 and 1644, the Dutch explorer Abel Tasman sailed around Australia and New Zealand.

On April 29, 1770, the Englishman Captain James Cook landed at Botany Bay in Australia.

Lewis and Clark

In 1803, President Thomas Jefferson bought a big piece of land in North America from the French. He asked Meriwether Lewis and William Clark to explore it and to find a route to the west coast of North America.

Rocky Mountains

DISCOVERY FACT™

Grizzly bears attacked the expedition in the Rocky Mountains. One bear chased six men into a river.

Lewis and Clark's **expedition** had to cross the Rocky Mountains. They spent one winter with a friendly **Native American** tribe called the Mandan.

The expedition reached the Pacific coast in November 1805. It had taken two years to cross the American **continent**.

The Mandan

Lewis and Clark

Australian Outback

DISCOVERY FACT™

Australian travelers used camels to help them travel through the Outback.

Crossing Australia

In 1860, the South Australian **government** offered a prize to the first person to travel across the Australian continent from the south coast to the north coast.

John McDouall Stuart

The center of Australia is hard to travel through because it is so hot and dry. It is called the Outback.

John McDouall Stuart made three attempts to cross Australia.

The north coast

In October 1861, McDouall Stuart reached the north coast of Australia. The continent had been crossed at last!

David Livingstone

David Livingstone was one of the greatest European explorers of Africa.

Livingstone lived in Africa for more than 30 years. He made four great journeys. He died during his final journey.

Livingstone came from a poor family in Scotland. He was a doctor and a **missionary** as well as an explorer.

Livingstone discovered new lakes and made the first maps of many rivers. He was the first European to see a waterfall that is now famous. He named it Victoria Falls after Queen Victoria.

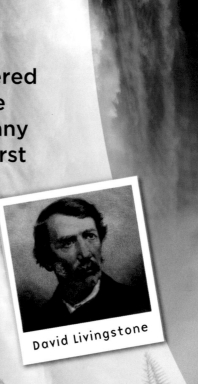

David Livingstone

DISCOVERY FACT™

Henry Stanley was an American **journalist**. In 1871, he traveled over 700 miles to find and talk to Livingstone.

Victoria Falls

DISCOVERY FACT™

Arctic and Antarctic explorers used husky dogs to pull sleds. Husky dogs have thick fur. They can survive very cold weather.

Race to the Poles

The **North Pole** is in the Arctic. The **South Pole** is in the Antarctic. In both places, it is very cold and dangerous.

Robert Peary

In 1909, American Robert Peary's team were probably the first people to reach the North Pole.

In 1911, two teams raced to the South Pole. The Englishman Robert Scott led one team. The Norwegian Roald Amundsen led the other team. Amundsen won the race.

Scott and his team all died on the journey back. They were not well enough prepared for the cold weather.

Scott's team

Quiz

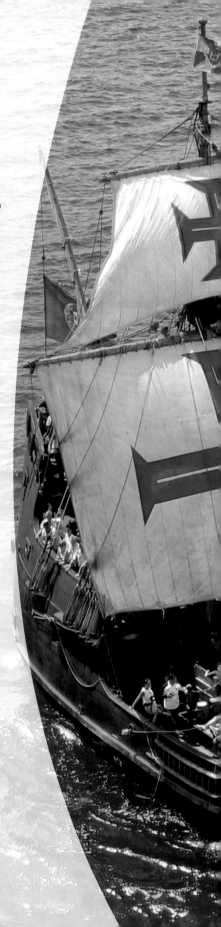

Now try this quiz!
All the answers can be
found in this book.

1. Who were the first
Europeans to visit
North America?

a) The Spanish
b) The English
c) The Vikings

2. Where did the Polo
family travel to?

a) America
b) Australia
c) China

3. Where was
Columbus trying
to sail to?

a) Africa
b) America
c) Asia

4. What mountains did Lewis and Clark have to cross?

a) The Himalayan Mountains
b) The Rocky Mountains
c) The Andes Mountains

5. What is the center of Australia called?

a) The Outback
b) The Australian Desert
c) The Great Space

6. Who was the first person to reach the South Pole?

a) Robert Scott
b) Roald Amundsen
c) Robert Peary

Glossary

Aborigine   The people who lived in Australia before Europeans arrived.

Continent   A big mass of land. Earth has seven continents. They are Europe, North America, South America, Asia, Oceania, Africa, and Antarctica.

Empire   A very large area of the world ruled by one government. The person who rules an empire is called an emperor or an empress.

European   Someone who comes from the continent of Europe.

Expedition   A difficult journey.

Government   The group of people who run a country.

Journalist   Someone who writes for a newspaper or magazine.

Missionary   A person who travels to another country to convert the local people to his or her religion.

Native American   The people who lived in the Americas before Europeans arrived.

North Pole   The North Pole is the very top of the earth.

Polynesian   The people who live on the islands in the Pacific Ocean.

Replica   An exact copy or model of something.

South Pole   The South Pole is the very bottom of the earth.

Index

Acknowledgments

Images from Corbis, Dreamstime, Getty Images, and iStockphoto